EXPLORING LATIN AMERICA

THE PEOPLE AND CULTURE OF LATIN AMERICA

D1716908

SUSAN NICHOLS

Britannica
Educational Publishing

IN ASSOCIATION WITH

ROSEN
EDUCATIONAL SERVICES

Published in 2018 by Britannica Educational Publishing (a trademark of Encyclopædia Britannica, Inc.) in association with The Rosen Publishing Group, Inc.
29 East 21st Street, New York, NY 10010

Distributed exclusively by Rosen Publishing.
To see additional Britannica Educational Publishing titles, go to rosenpublishing.com.

First Edition

Britannica Educational Publishing
J.E. Luebering: Executive Director, Core Editorial
Andrea R. Field: Managing Editor, Compton's by Britannica

Rosen Publishing
Carolyn DeCarlo: Editor
Nelson Sá: Art Director
Michael Moy: Series Designer
Raúl Rodriguez: Book Layout
Cindy Reiman: Photography Manager
Nicole Baker: Photo Researcher

Library of Congress Cataloging-in-Publication Data

Names: Nichols, Susan, 1975- author.
Title: The people and culture of Latin America / Susan Nichols.
Description: New York : Britannica Educational Publishing in Association with Rosen Educational Services, 2018. | Series: Exploring Latin America | Audience: Grades 5-8. | Includes bibliographical references and index.
Identifiers: LCCN 2017001516| ISBN 9781680486919 (library bound : alkaline paper) | ISBN 9781680486896 (paperback : alkaline paper) | ISBN 9781680486902 (6 pack : alkaline paper)
Subjects: LCSH: Latin America—Social life and customs—Juvenile literature.
| Latin America—Intellectual life—Juvenile literature. | Latin America—Social conditions—Juvenile literature.
Classification: LCC F1408.3 .N49 2017 | DDC 980—dc23
LC record available at https://lccn.loc.gov/2017001516

Manufactured in the United States of America

CONTENTS

INTRODUCTION

In 1982, the Nobel Prize for Literature was awarded to Gabriel García Márquez, the Colombian author of such celebrated novels as *One Hundred Years of Solitude* and *Love in the Time of Cholera*. Márquez, in an interview with the *New York Times*, expressed some anxiety about being given the coveted award. Even though he was not the first writer from Latin America to receive it, he feared that he would be called on to represent Latin America.

"I must try and break through the clichés about Latin America," he said in his interview. "Superpowers and other outsiders have fought over us for centuries in ways that have nothing to do with our problems. In reality, we are all alone."

Márquez was referring to the way in which Latin American culture is often misunderstood and misrepresented. Latin America is much more diverse and dynamic than some people have assumed.

Gabriel García Márquez, Colombian novelist and winner of the Nobel Prize

The term "Latin America" might sound strange, since Latin is not spoken in this region. However, the term is over 150 years old and was invented to refer to the region

LOUISIANA
to New Spain 1763
(Audiencia
of Cuba)   St. Louis

BRITISH
TERRITORY

San Francisco

*ATLANTIC
OCEAN*   30°

**VICEROYALTY
OF NEW SPAIN**

*Gulf of
Mexico*   Havana

CUBA

Mexico City

Santo Domingo

Acapulco

C a r i b b e a n   S e a

Guatemala City

Cartagena   Caracas

Panama

Bogotá   GUIANA

**VICEROYALTY OF
NEW GRANADA**

Equator   0°

Quito

Pará

**VICEROYALTY
OF BRAZIL**   Recife

Lima   Cuzco   Salvador

**VICEROYALTY
OF PERU**

Potosí

Rio de
Janeiro

*PACIFIC
OCEAN*

**VICEROYALTY
OF THE RÍO DE
LA PLATA**   30°

Santiago

Montevideo
Buenos Aires

Spanish and Portuguese
America 1780

——— border between Portuguese
      and Spanish territory 1750

- - - border amended 1778

PATAGONIA

0   600   1200 mi

0   900   1800 km
© 2009 Encyclopædia Britannica, Inc.   90°   75°   60°   45°

A map of the Americas in 1780 shows the four Spanish viceroyalties
in green and Portuguese territory (Brazil) in purple.

5

located south of the border of the United States because these countries and dependent states speak languages derived from Latin: Spanish, Portuguese, and French. Even the other languages, such as Creole languages spoken in the West Indies, are a fusion of Latin languages with other tongues, such as African languages.

Latin American nations are the southern neighbors of the United States. However, the population of Latin America is much greater than that of the United States. For example, the United States has approximately 325 million people within its borders. In contrast, Brazil alone has approximately 205 million people! It is the fifth most populous country in the world, and one-third of the people of Latin America live there.

Altogether, more than 626 million people live in Latin America, a region that covers some 15 percent of the

The skyline of Panama City, the capital and largest city of Panama

Earth. The people and cultures are as diverse as the region itself, which includes Mexico, Central America, South America, and the West Indies—areas with vastly different features. The West Indies and Caribbean are islands, for example, that enjoy a tropical climate. On the other hand, many nations on the western side of South America are marked by the Andes Mountains and enjoy cooler climates. In yet another example, many Central and South American cities are built on coastlines—bordering either the Atlantic, the Pacific, or the Gulf of Mexico—and those regions are influenced by that feature.

While these countries are diverse in many ways (for example, Brazilian culture differs from Peruvian culture, which differs from Cuban culture), they all have certain broader attributes in common. These similarities have been influenced by their shared history.

CHAPTER ONE

INDIGENOUS ROOTS

When Christopher Columbus landed in the Americas in 1492, he opened the way for European colonization of what came to be known as the New World. The lands he encountered, however, had long been populated by Amerindians, the indigenous people of North and South America. In fact, cultures dating back at least thirteen thousand years already existed on the two "new" continents and neighboring islands of the Americas.

The indigenous people were diverse in many ways. They had different languages, religions, systems of government, and traditions. At the time of the European conquest of Latin America, the three major indigenous civilizations—or "high civilizations"—were the Maya of Mesoamerica, the Aztecs of Mexico, and the Incas of Peru.

THREE HIGH CIVILIZATIONS

The Mayan culture flourished between 1000 BCE and 1542 CE. Mayan corn farmers grew the vegetable in abundance,

An eighth-century terra-cotta Mayan sculpture from Mexico depicting a deity who was worshiped as part of the cult of the corn

TELLING TIME

The Mayan and Aztec civilizations were sophisticated and highly developed, and they had many remarkable achievements. Mayan priests, for example, created a calendar—a system for dating time—that became the basis for all other systems used by ancient Mexican and Central American civilizations.

The Mayan calendar featured a cycle of 365 days, which ran concurrently with a cycle of 260 named days. The named days were believed to have certain fateful characteristics, while the unnamed days were considered extremely unlucky, prompting the Maya to fast or honor the gods with sacrifices on those days. The calendar was divided into

A page from the Dresden Codex, a thirteenth-century Mayan manuscript containing astronomical tables

eighteen months of twenty days each, and one extra month of five days. The calendar also featured a longer cycle of 18,980 days, or fifty-two years of 365 days (the longer cycle was called the "Calendar Round" by the Maya).

Each day in the calendar was noted in a sophisticated and complex way; it was identified by four characteristics: 1) the day number, 2) the day name in the 260-day cycle, 3) the day number within the month, and 4) the month name in the 365-day cycle.

The Aztecs used the same structure as the Mayan calendar. They created elaborate rituals to celebrate and honor the gods of each of the particular named days. They also had a celebration of the time when, every 52 years, the cycles in the calendar were "reset" to their original position. This celebration was known as the "Binding Up of the Years," or the New Fire Ceremony. All ritual fires were allowed to burn out, and then Aztec priests would light a new sacred fire on the chest of a sacrificial victim. The Aztec people would use this new flame to light fires in their homes.

supplying much of the food for Mayan cities and towns. Perhaps because food was in large supply, the Mayans had time and leisure to focus on art and religion. Examples of Mayan artwork and architecture can be found in the ruins of their cities, such as Tikal. Mayan priests managed temples and religious sites and managed the Mayan calendar. About two million Mayan Indians live in northern Yucatán and Guatemala today—their lives a close imitation of their ancestors'.

The Aztecs emerged as a people in Mexico as early as 1200 CE, and their civilization flourished, becoming powerful and advanced. When Hernán Cortés and the Spanish conquistadors discovered their capital, Tenochtitlán, they were amazed by its huge white palaces and ornate temples on pyramids. A culture that celebrated religion, the Aztec priests devised an accurate solar calendar, and they created an almanac that listed dates for various festivals and documented which gods were responsible for certain times of the year. The Aztecs spoke the Nahuan language. Mexico City is built on the ruins of Tenochtitlán, and the Indians living in the Mexico City region today

An Aztec priest performs a sacrificial offering of a living human heart to the war god Huitzilopochtli. This illustration is from a reproduction of the Codex Magliabecchi.

70

are descendants of the Aztecs.

The Incas of Peru had similarly built an impressive civilization. While they had no form of writing, they used a system of knotted cords, called *quipus*, to keep records and assess taxes. The language of the Inca Empire was Quechua. Today, South American Indians living in the Andean highlands from Ecuador to Bolivia still speak many regional varieties of Quechua.

A bookkeeper rendering accounts to the Inca ruler. The storehouses' contents are recorded on his quipu.

Alongside these three civilizations, the Arawak Native Americans lived on the islands of the Caribbean Sea and in northern South America. Their language was also called Arawak, and those who lived on the island of Hispaniola (currently known as Haiti and the Dominican Republic) were the first indigenous peoples that Columbus met. Most of the Arawak population died after the Spanish conquest, but a small number still exist in South America, in Guyana as well as in Suriname, French Guiana, and Venezuela.

THE CHANGING FACE OF LATIN AMERICA

Historians agree that the European colonization of Latin America, which began with the conquest of the Spanish, radically changed the people and culture of the region. Many countries were part of the colonization: Spain, Portugal, France, England and the Dutch Republic. Additionally, many colonists settled in the new colonies and never returned to their original countries. Some married indigenous people or had children with indigenous women, which changed the ethnic makeup of the region even further.

Significantly, colonists usually participated in the trans-Atlantic slave trade, which forcibly brought Africans to South America to labor as slaves on the land. In this way, a once-indigenous Latin America became a home to three races: the native Americans, the Europeans, and the Africans.

CHAPTER TWO

LIVING IN LATIN AMERICA

Where and how do most people in Latin America live? Approximately one-third of Latin Americans live in Brazil, the most populated country in the region. Another one-fifth live in Mexico, just south of the United States. And most of those people live in the urban areas of those two nations. In fact, Mexico City and São

An aerial view of Mexico City, the capital of Mexico. Mexico City is densely populated, with almost nine million people living within its boundaries.

Paulo, Brazil, have grown to become two of the world's largest metropolitan areas.

Overall, cities in Latin America have been growing rapidly since the 1940s; the suburbs and rural areas of many Latin American nations have been swallowed up by the expanding borders of these cities. Initially, people moved to the cities to find jobs as their countries—Mexico and Brazil, in particular—found their footing in the international marketplace as manufacturing centers. Currently, four-fifths of Latin Americans live in cities. According to Brazilian journalist Paulo A. Paranagua, "By 2050, 90 percent of Latin America's population will be in towns and cities. Brazil and the southern cone may reach this level by 2020."

THE LENS OF POVERTY

Unfortunately, many people who have moved to these behemoth cities have not seen their lives improve. Poverty is a major problem in Latin American cities. To be clear, there are some very wealthy people, but there are also incredibly poor people—and often, they live not far from each other in the same city.

The poorest part of the populace—over 100 million—live in "shantytowns," or settlements in which people create their own housing out of whatever materials are available. These houses are usually shacks or other non-sturdy structures. This makes their homes more vulnerable to natural disasters such as hurricanes and earthquakes. On January 12, 2010, a major earthquake hit the island of Hispaniola, which is home to both Haiti and the Dominican Republic. The earthquake hit 15 miles away from Haiti's main city,

Port-au-Prince, and Haitians suffered the most; it is estimated that almost 300,000 people died, while over one million Haitians were left homeless by the earthquake.

Studies have found that with poverty comes urban violence. According to Paranagua, "Latin American cities are the most unequal and often most dangerous places in the world." Crime levels are very high, and many people are jobless.

The economies of these Latin American countries are still "developing," which means that the average jobholder working in Latin America does not earn as much as they would in a country with a more established economic system. The average income of a citizen of the United States is six times higher than that of a citizen of Argentina or Mexico, for example. Despite this, the range of incomes across

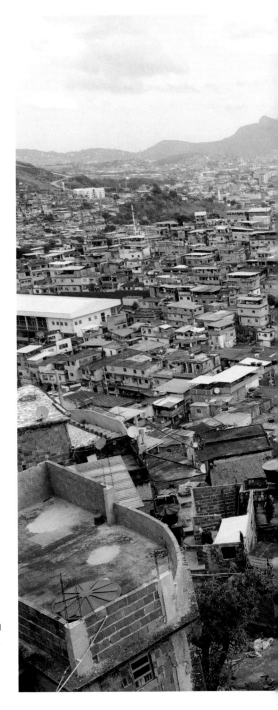

A panoramic view of an urban slum in Rio de Janeiro, in Brazil

OLYMPIC-SIZED BENEFITS?

The Summer Olympic Games, one of the most anticipated sporting events in the world, were held in Rio de Janeiro, Brazil, in 2016. It is an honor to be chosen to host the Olympics, and cities around the world compete to be able to hold the events in their own backyards. Being a host city for the Olympics brings many benefits to a city and a nation, because the top athletes from around the world converge on that city for the competitions, which include events in a range of sports from swimming to shooting, soccer to gymnastics, among many others. The media attention of the world is focused on that city for several weeks, placing a spotlight on the city and nation as a whole.

It is very expensive to host the Olympics. Most nations usually build at least one building to house the tournaments and events. In 2012, London built several structures, including the Olympics Stadium and the Velodrome. Every two years, people question whether the host nation of the Summer or Winter Olympics has enough money to host the competition. No exception, in 2016 many people questioned whether Brazil, which suffers from high levels of poverty, could afford to play host to the Olympics. According to Michael Dobie of *Newsday*, Brazil spent $11 billion to host the Summer Games. Some journalists argued that the average Brazilian citizen would not be able to afford the price of a ticket to attend some of the events.

There were also concerns about crime and violence. Many international athletes were worried about spending time in Rio de Janeiro, because street crime rates were high. The Brazilian government promised to step up security forces and the police presence during the Games—which it did. But Brazilians protested that they, as citizens, were paying for the costs of the increased security with their own tax money.

A scenic view of the beautiful Atlantic coastline of Rio de Janeiro, Brazil

Latin America is quite wide—a person's income is still ten times higher on average in Mexico than someone who lives in Haiti or Nicaragua.

EDUCATIONAL HIGHS AND LOWS

Despite the poverty of Latin American countries, the school systems in place tend to be quite good—even though many public schools are underfunded. Unfortunately, about half of children are not enrolled in secondary schools and

Mosaic mural by David Alfaro Siqueiros, 1952–53, on the Central Administration Building at University City, Mexico City

therefore do not get the opportunity to take advantage of the educational opportunities surrounding them.

The university system in Latin America is very strong academically. There are many renowned universities, such as the National Autonomous University of Mexico in Mexico City and the University of São Paulo in Brazil.

CHAPTER THREE

RELIGION AND TRADITION IN LATIN AMERICA

One of the lasting influences on Latin American people and their cultures comes from their European colonizers. Recall that the original Spanish conquistadors had a twofold mission: to get rich and to convert the native Americans to Roman Catholicism. During this period of colonization in the New World, many indigenous people were forced to convert to Roman Catholicism, as were the Africans brought against their will to Latin America as slaves. As a direct result, approximately 70 to 95 percent of people in Latin America today are Christian. Of these, 90 percent are Roman Catholic—although Protestant denominations, especially Evangelical churches, have grown in popularity.

HOLY DAYS IN LATIN AMERICA

Many Latin Americans celebrate Christian holidays, including Christmas, the recognized birthday of Jesus of Nazareth, founder of the Christian faith. Sometimes, these celebrations involve traditions that would be unfamiliar to

Christmas decorations at the Parque Norte ("North Park") in Medellin, Colombia

outsiders of these cultures and their individual contexts. In some Latin American countries, including El Salvador, Christmas is marked by launching fireworks! In Panama, Christians celebrate by making and decorating a life-sized doll called a *muñeca*, which looks like themselves or family members. Many Latin Americans also enjoy building elaborate Nativity scenes that replicate the birth of Jesus in a manger in Bethlehem; these scenes include the baby Jesus, Mary his mother, Joseph her husband, several animals, three wise men, and the angel Gabriel.

In Latin America, another major religious holiday is Easter, the feast day that commemorates Jesus' resurrection, or rising from the dead. The entire week before Easter Sunday is known as Holy Week, or *Semana Santa*, and is one of the most important holidays in Latin American nations. Semana Santa starts on Palm Sunday, or *Domingo de Ramos*, and ends with Easter Sunday, or *Domingo de Resurrección*. In many countries, people walk in ceremonial processions, in which they carry images of Christ, and attend Mass at their local church. Many people also fast on Good Friday, or *Viernes Santo*, the day recognized for Jesus' death, to mark the sadness of the occasion.

BLENDED CULTURES, BLENDED RELIGIONS

Many Latin Americans practice religions that are forms of syncretism. This means that they blend two or more different belief systems into a new form. For example, Santería is a popular religion in Cuba. "Santería" means "The Way of the Saints," and it is a fusion of West African Yoruba religious traditions with Roman Catholic creed. It is a way that many Africans preserved their religious heritage upon being brought against their will to Latin America to work as slaves.

In Haiti, the African religious legacy can be seen in the popularity of Voodoo, also known as Vodou, another syncretic religion. Voodoo blends Roman Catholicism, Yoruba and Congo traditions, as well as Taino (a group of Arawak indigenous peoples) beliefs from the Caribbean. In Jamaica, the Obeah religion is often compared

SANTERÍA

Although most Latin Americans are Christians, syncretic religions are also popular. One syncretic religion that has a great number of adherents is Santería, which means "The Way of the Saints." It is a fusion of West African and Catholic traditions that emerged from the slave trade on the island of Cuba in the Caribbean.

What do Santeríans believe? They believe that there is a chief god, Olodumare, as well as spirits known as orishas. The orishas can help humans achieve their full potential and live happy lives, which is why humans should worship them. However, orishas are mortal, and so they need sacrifices to be made to them to survive, especially animal sacrifices to feed the spirits.

Adherents offer sacrifices for several reasons, such as weddings, funerals, or moments of difficulty or crisis, such as illness. The person who makes the sacrifice will eat the meat of the animal, believing that the blood is for the orisha.

Santeríans also practice a ceremony known as "bembe," in which, through drumming and dancing, adherents invite the orisha to join them and guide them.

Yoruba women in Africa perform a traditional dance, influential to the Santeríans in Cuba.

Adherents of the Voodoo religion bathe in a sacred pool during the annual Voodoo festival held during Easter weekend in Souvenance, Haiti.

to Haitian Voodoo. People who adhere to this practice believe that potions or other items have spiritual power to ward off evil.

In Brazil, two popular religions are Umbanda and Candomblé. Both of these faiths blend Roman Catholicism, South American indigenous beliefs, and *macumba*, which means "magic." Macumba is inherited from Brazil's African population, and it is marked by animal sacrifices and spiritual offerings.

In South America, there are also small communities that practice Islam, Judaism, Hinduism, and Buddhism. Many of these adherents are immigrants, but also include converts to these faiths.

CHAPTER FOUR

RACE, ETHNICITY, AND LANGUAGE

Even though Latin Americans have some common characteristics—vibrant native, indigenous cultures; the conversion of a majority of the population to Christianity; and the shared history of European colonialism—they are diverse in many other ways, including race, ethnicity, and language.

A MIXED HERITAGE

A range of racial and ethnic groups have developed and sustained across the region. Indigenous groups, represented by many individual and distinct tribes, remain prevalent in Latin America; they are the original inhabitants of South America and the Caribbean. White people remain, as descendants of the Europeans, as well as Africans, descended from the people who were forced into slavery during the slave trade in Latin America.

Most Latin Americans identify themselves as *mestizos*, or "biracial"—they are usually of mixed European and

A Zapotec Indian woman in Ocotlan, Mexico. Members of indigenous groups are descended from the original inhabitants of the Americas and the Caribbean.

indigenous heritage. Sometimes, in Central America, mestizos refer to themselves as *Ladinos*. Others identify as *mulattos*, or people of mixed European and African heritage.

There are also some communities in Latin America who are South Asian; these groups are especially prominent in countries like Guyana, Trinidad, and Suriname. One can find people of Japanese and Chinese ancestry in communities across Brazil, Peru, Mexico, and Cuba.

LANGUAGE: A UNIFYING INHERITANCE

The language of Latin America is predominantly Spanish, which is an inheritance of Spain's colonialism of the region and spoken by 400 million people. In contrast, in Brazil, which was colonized by Portugal, the dominant language is Portuguese. Because of the large population of Brazil, Portuguese is the most frequently spoken language on the South American continent, spoken by 200 million people. English is also a widely spoken language in the region.

Although French and Creole are spoken by smaller numbers of Latin

Signs written in Portuguese and English line the interior of the Maracana stadium in Rio de Janeiro, Brazil.

HAITIAN CREOLE

In countries like Haiti, the dominant language is Creole, which is based on French; France was one of the European powers that had colonized Hispaniola.

According to linguistics scholar Albert Valdman, "The term creole comes from a Portuguese word meaning 'raised in the home.' It first referred to Europeans born and raised in the overseas colonies. It was later used for languages that arose on the plantations that the Europeans established." Indeed, Haitian Creole developed as a way for

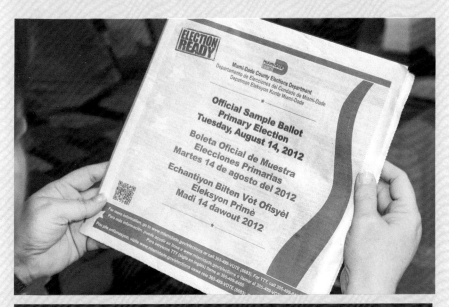

Alongside English and Spanish, Haitian Creole appears on sample ballots in Miami Beach, Florida—a sign of the growing Haitian American community in the area.

(continued on the next page)

(continued from the previous page)

French slaveowners to communicate with their African slaves. The slaves came from various regions in Africa, and they often arrived on slave ships speaking a variety of languages. These languages melded together, fused with the informal French of the slave masters, and a new language was born.

Currently, Creole is spoken by more than 95 percent of Haitians—approximately ten million people—plus another one million Haitians who live outside of Hispaniola. It was recognized in 1987 as one of Haiti's official languages. This is rare; many Latin American nations use a creole language, blended with French. The difference is that in Haiti, Creole is not a dialect, it is a formal language used in schools, government, and other official settings.

Americans—approximately eight million—these languages are more significant in the Caribbean. In countries like Argentina, one can also hear German being spoken. In Guyana, which is located on South America's northern Atlantic coast, Hindu and Urdu are spoken among the members of the South Asian community. In Trinidad and Tobago, two nations that share an island off the coast of Venezuela, Chinese is also spoken in some communities.

Many indigenous groups have held onto their cultures and languages in the face of European colonialism, and their languages have survived. In Peru, Ecuador, and Bolivia, for example, Quechua and Aymara are spoken, while one can hear the Nahuatl language spoken in Mexico and Mayan languages in Central America.

CHAPTER FIVE

THE LITERATURE AND ART OF LATIN AMERICA

Latin American culture is as innovative and as diverse as its people. Many renowned artists, writers, and musicians, both past and present, from across Latin America have inspired people around the world.

BOLD BRUSHSTROKES

In the art world, Roberto Matta from Chile is renowned for his abstract expressionist and surrealist work. Known popularly as "Matta," he was born in Santiago, Chile, in 1911. He became friends with acclaimed writers such as Federico García Lorca and Pablo Neruda, who introduced him to European artists like Salvador Dalí and André Breton. He was invited to join a group of Surrealist artists in 1937. He became known for blending political and social commentary into his artistic work, especially in a series of art known collectively as *El Mediterráneo y el verbo América*.

One of the most popular artists from Latin America was the muralist Diego Rivera, whose fame might be rivalled

A 1978 photograph shows Chilean artist Roberto Matta, standing in the hall of Chilean artists under construction at the Biennale, in Venice, Italy.

only by that of his wife, the masterful painter Frida Kahlo. Rivera was born in Guanajuato, Mexico in 1886, and at only ten years old he was sent to study art at the San Carlos Academy of Fine Arts in Mexico City. He became dedicated to the idea of creating art that represented the lives and aspirations of the Mexican people. This is because he was personally moved by the Mexican Revolution (1910–20) and he was proud that Mexico was on the path to overthrowing tyranny and embracing freedom. One of his most popular works is a series of murals in Mexico City that celebrate Mexican history, titled *From the Pre-Hispanic Civilization to the Conquest.*

Matta, Rivera, and Kahlo—as well as many other Latin American artists—were internationally known and celebrated. Their work influenced many other artists around the world. But it is equally important to point out that many Latin American artists produce work that is locally revered and no less significant. For example, many indigenous artists have produced beautiful pottery, wood carvings, ceremonial masks, paintings, and other work that is categorized as "folk art"—the art of the people.

A RICH LITERARY TRADITION

Latin American literature is also celebrated and has been influential on both a local and international level. Many Latin American writers have been awarded the Nobel Prize in Literature, including Gabriela Mistral (Chile), Miguel Ángel Asturias (Guatemala), Pablo Neruda (Chile), Gabriel García Márquez (Colombia), Octavio Paz (Mexico), and Mario Vargas Llosa (Peru). There are many other

FEMINIST ART

Fellow Mexican painter Frida Kahlo is recognized as Diego Rivera's equal in talent and artistic sensibility. Kahlo was born in 1907 in Coyoacán, Mexico. As a little girl, she contracted polio, which she survived but which caused her to walk with a limp. Later, as a young woman, she was terribly injured in a bus accident that left her spine and pelvis damaged. She began painting while recuperating from this accident, and the subject of most of her paintings was herself. She created self-portraits that revealed deeply personal and emotional facets of her life. Her work was displayed in Europe and the United States, and her fame has only grown in the years since her death. Indeed, she is now considered a feminist icon because she focused on asserting her own ideas and themes in her artwork. She refused, throughout her life, to allow her husband Rivera's work to overshadow hers.

A photograph of Mexican artists Frida Kahlo and Diego Rivera, who were married

contemporary writers who are popular today, both in Latin America and abroad. They include Chilean writers Alejandro Zambra and Roberto Bolaño—whose work has been lauded since his untimely death in 2003—Edwidge Danticat (Haiti), and Paulo Coelho (Brazil).

One of the most popular literary trends that has emerged from Latin America is known as "magic realism," a literary style in fiction that blends realistic events with fantastical elements in a very particular way. Two of its greatest proponents were Colombian writer Gabriel García Márquez and the Argentinian Jorge Luis Borges. Isabel Allende, a Chilean who was born in 1942 in Lima, Peru, is also known for her use of magic realism, particularly in her novel *The House of the Spirits*. She has also written a moving memoir, *Paula*, about the life and death of her daughter.

Latin American writers also pioneered other writing styles, including experimental narratives in which the story is told in a nonlinear fashion. Jorge Luis Borges is most famous for this method. Born in 1899 in Buenos Aires, Borges spent some of his teenage years in Switzerland. He returned to Latin America and began writing poetry and short stories. He experimented with length and forms: in fact, one of his stories, "On Exactitude in Science," is only one paragraph long. Many of his stories are told in a fragmented way, where the reader has to piece together what is happening. Borges' themes are philosophical and ask questions about the meaning of life and reality; for example, some of his main characters are writers who are reflecting on writing as a process.

President Barack Obama presents the Presidential Medal of Freedom to author Isabel Allende at the White House on November 24, 2014, in Washington, DC.

A MASTER OF MAGIC REALISM

Gabriel García Márquez, born in Aracataca, Colombia, in 1927, is one of the most renowned writers who wrote in the style of magic realism. He was awarded the Nobel Prize for Literature in 1982. Some of his most well-known novels include *One Hundred Years of Solitude* and *Love in the Time of Cholera*.

In his work, Márquez celebrates the lives of everyday people in Colombia. His famous short story "A Very Old Man with Enormous Wings" highlights this aspect of the genre. In it, an old, injured man is found by the main character:

> He was dressed like a ragpicker. There were only a few faded hairs left on his bald skull and very few teeth in his mouth, and his pitiful condition of a drenched great-grandfather took away any sense of grandeur he might have had. His huge buzzard wings, dirty and half-plucked, were forever entangled in the mud.

Here, the man is depicted realistically overall; the fact that he has wings growing out of his back is treated as just one more detail, despite it being something that is imaginary.

Celia Cruz, photographed here in 1962, was a Cuban American singer who reigned for decades as the "Queen of Salsa Music."

MUSICAL INNOVATORS

Like the art and literature of the region, Latin American music combines indigenous, European, and African influences. In Cuba, the African influence is evident in *afrocubanismo*-style music. Musicians use instruments and rhythms to create a new, exciting style of music. Some of the well-known musicians include Alejandro García Caturla, who was born in 1906 in Remedios, Cuba, where he spent most of his life. He is known as one of the most important composers of the last century for his imaginative, lyrical pieces, which include *Tres Danzas Cubanas* and *Bembe*.

Domingo Santa Cruz, a Chilean musician and composer, was born in 1899. He founded many musical institutions and organizations that promoted Chilean-style music, including the Bach Society, Revista Musical Chilena, and the Extension Institute of Fine Arts.

Many styles of music have connections to or origins in Latin America, including salsa and Tejano music. Reggae music originated in Jamaica, while bomba and plena are hallmarks of Puerto Rican music. The cultures of Trinidad and Tobago gave rise to the emergence of calypso and soca music.

Latin America's literary, artistic, and musical traditions are vibrant and energetic, and they draw strength from the region's diverse population and history.

GLOSSARY

bomba A style of music popular in Puerto Rico.

Calendar Round A system of days in a fifty-two-year cycle that is a feature of the Mayan calendar.

colonialism A system of oppression and occupation by one national power over another.

Creole A fusion of French and African languages that is spoken in the Caribbean.

indigenous Relating to the original, native people of Latin America.

macumba A religion practiced in Brazil.

magic realism A style of writing, blending realistic details with imagination and fantasy, that was popularized by Latin American writers.

mestizo A person whose ancestry includes indigenous and European heritage.

mulatto A person whose ancestry includes European and African heritage.

muñeca A life-sized doll that is part of a Panamanian Christmas tradition.

murals Art forms in which large paintings use large spaces, especially walls, as a canvas.

Obeah A religion that is popular in the Caribbean.

orishas Spirits worshipped by adherents of the Santería faith.

plena A musical style that is popular in Puerto Rico.

quipus System of knotted cords used by the Inca civilization to keep records and assess taxes.

reggae A musical style that is popular in Jamaica.

Roman Catholicism A denomination of Christianity that follows the guidance of the pope in Rome, Italy.

salsa A musical style that developed largely in the United States but has roots in Latin America.

Santería A religion popular in Cuba that blends Catholicism with African Yoruba traditions.

shantytowns Settlements, in which houses are constructed of often non-sturdy materials, inhabited by the poor.

Semana Santa The Holy Week before Easter.

soca A musical style that originated in the Caribbean.

surrealism A twentieth-century style of art and literature that sought to tap into the thought processes of the unconscious mind.

syncretism Relating to the blending of cultures and traditions, as in the syncretic religions of Latin American that blend European, indigenous, and African beliefs.

Voodoo A religion that combines traditional African beliefs with elements of Roman Catholicism and is practiced chiefly in Haiti.

FOR FURTHER READING

Engle, Margarita. *Enchanted Air: Two Cultures, Two Wings: A Memoir*. New York, NY: Atheneum Books for Young Readers, 2016.

Farnsworth-Alvear, Ann, Marco Palacios, and Ana María Gómez López. *The Colombia Reader: History, Culture, Politics*. Durham, NC: Duke University Press, 2016.

Forrest, John, and Julia Porturas. *Peru* (Culture Smart!: The Essential Guide to Customs & Culture). London, UK: Kuperard Publishers, 2012.

Gofen, Ethel. *Argentina: Cultures of the World*. New York, NY: Cavendish Publishers, 2012.

Keen, Benjamin, and Keith Haynes. *A History of Latin America*, 9th Edition. Boston, MA: Cengage Learning, 2012.

Ng Cheong-Lum, Roseline. *Haiti* (Cultures of the World). New York, NY: Cavendish Publishers, 2016.

Peppas, Lynn. *Cultural Traditions in Jamaica*. New York, NY: Crabtree Publishing, 2015.

Shields, Charles. *El Salvador* (Discovering Central America: History, Politics, and Culture). Broomall, PA: Mason Crest Publishers, 2015.

WEBSITES

Because of the changing nature of internet links, Rosen Publishing has developed an online list of websites related to the subject of this book. This site is updated regularly. Please use this link to access this list:

http://www.rosenlinks.com/ELA/people

INDEX